SMOKERS' HUMOUR

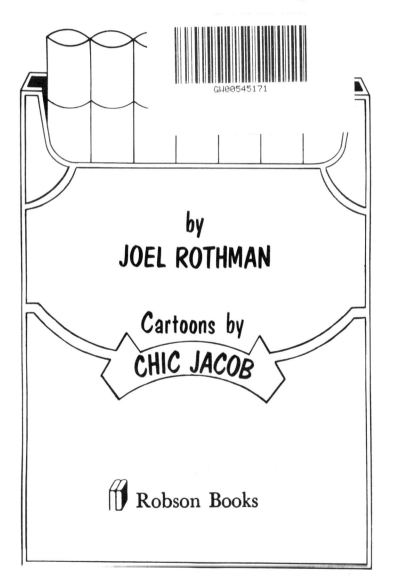

by
JOEL ROTHMAN

Cartoons by
CHIC JACOB

Robson Books

FIRST PUBLISHED IN GREAT BRITAIN IN 1983
BY ROBSON BOOKS LTD., BOLSOVER HOUSE,
5-6 CLIPSTONE STREET, LONDON W1P 7EB.
COPYRIGHT © 1983 J.R. PUBLICATIONS
INCORPORATED

British Library Cataloguing in Publication Data

Rotham, Joel
Smokers' humour.
1. Smoking — Anecdotes, facetiae, satire, etc.
I. Title
613.8'5'0207   HV5726

ISBN 0-86051-218-5

Printed in Hungary

Cigarette: A fire at one end, a fool at the other, and a bit of tobacco between.

Optimist — a husband who discovers cigar butts at the side of the bed, and assumes his wife has stopped smoking cigarettes.

You should treat a cigar like a mistress; put it away before you are sick of it.

Disraeli

I remember that first learning to inhale was just as difficult as trying to give up smoking.

An actor came home carrying a Christmas gift under his arm. He said to his wife, "I have purchased something for the one I love best. Can you guess what it is?"

"A box of cigars?" she asked.

When people give up smoking, they often substitute something for the cigarettes — usually it's an irritable disposition.

Ashtray —— a place to flick your ashes if you haven't got a floor.

Are people who manufacture cigarettes illegally called *butt-leggers?*

When it comes to agriculture, Thailand is quite an advanced country. The farmers usually rotate their crops — opium one year, hashish the next.

Remember — thousands of people have quit smoking, but not one has died because of it.

I don't like to complain about the price of cigarettes, but yesterday I went into a tobacconist's to buy a few packs and said to the assistant, "I'm sorry, but I only have a £10 note."

He told me, "That's okay — you can pay me the rest the next time you're passing by."

My grandfather loves to recall when you could buy a good ten-pence cigar for ten pence, but forgets that he worked a twelve-hour day.

A family that smokes together, chokes together.

It's almost impossible to find one spouse, one friend, or one cigarette lighter you can depend upon.

The man who turns over a new leaf has probably changed his brand of cigars.

One group who should cut down on smoking are those people who are constantly bumming cigarettes.

Some people smoke between meals — others eat between smokes.

One good way to help break the smoking habit is to light the filter end of the cigarette first.

Albert smoked three packets a day when he went to the doctor with a terrible cough and a sore throat. He pointed to his throat and said in a hoarse voice, "Cigarettes did this to me, doc."

"Smoking them?" asked the doctor.

"No," said Albert, "asking for them."

The curious thing about smoking is that it kills live men, but cures dead swine.

In order to help stop smoking, my neighbour tried studying yoga. It didn't get him to kick the habit, but now he's able to smoke standing on his head!

It is now proved beyond doubt that smoking is one of the leading causes of statistics.

Nobody can be so revoltingly smug as the man who has just given up smoking.